MW00860713

Dragonfly Haiku

Dragonfly Haiku

by

Kobayashi Issa

Ken Tennessen

Scott King

Red Dragonfly Press

English versions of Issa copyright © 2016 by Scott King
Text copyright © 2016 by Ken Tennessen
Introduction and text copyright © 2016 by Scott King
    All rights reserved

ISBN 978-1-937693-98-5

Grateful acknowledgment is made to the editors of *Great River Review* and the *Minnesota Dragonfly Society Newsletter* where several of these haiku were first published.

Eleven Issa versions were printed as a letterpress keepsake in 2014 for an evening of dragonfly poetry at the Lee & Rose Warner Nature Center with Scott King, Ron Lawrenz and John Caddy.

Designed and typeset by Scott King
    using Dante MT Std

Published by Red Dragonfly Press
    307 Oxford Street
    Northfield, MN 55057

www.reddragonflypress.org

CONTENTS

INTRODUCTION

"Listen: how is it
that our troubled voice mingles like this
with the stars?"
– Philippe Jaccottet, from 'To Henry Purcell'

Among the great insect philosophers and theoreticians
and poets I'm inclined to place, above most others,
Jean Henri Fabre, Harry Martinson, and Kobayashi Issa.
Fabre's true love was of the psammophilous insects,
especially the hunting wasps and the dung beetles that
dwelled near his home in Sérignan, in the south of France.
But he had, in addition, a wide knowledge of the natural
world, including dragonfly nymphs: "here, squalidly clad
in mud, is the grub of the largest of our Dragon-flies, so
curious because of its manner of progression: it fills its
hinder-parts, a yawning funnel, with water, spurts it out
again and advances just so far as the recoil of its hydraulic
cannon."

Harry Martinson, awarded a Nobel Prize for literature
in 1947, masterfully described insect and observer
interactions. The summer meadows of Sweden and those
of Wisconsin and Minnesota have much in common.
Here, for instance, in his late book of essays, *Views from a
Tuft of Grass*, he comes as close as anyone has to positing
solutions to the following questions: Why dragonflies?
Why poetry? Questions I've held a long time, and have
tried to answer over and over, in haiku after haiku.

"Such a distinctively emphasized experience of one spot, of one now and one life, can only be conveyed by insects, because they are small enough to make us focus our vision on that particular point in the living now. At the same time we find there is a different system of coordinates here than the one that deals with positions—a coordinate system of the senses, of experience and poetry.

There doesn't seem much we can do about the fact that we choose our favorite insects according to the way they look, and according to the intensity of their beauty. That is how we function."

This coordinate system agrees almost perfectly with the coordinate system of haiku, that is the intersection of exactness of language with accuracy of observation.

Kobayashi Issa (1763 - 1828), a lay priest of Shin Buddhism (the True Pure Land School), wrote over 20,000 haiku and is considered one of the great Japanese masters of the form. Noted for his humble, down-to-earth views of life, Issa wrote numerous poems about insects, granting equal status to such creatures as fleas and mosquitoes, celebrating the surprising behavior of cicadas, stink bugs (Issa calls them fart bugs), and butterflies. The ten annotated poems included here are chosen from the more than fifty he wrote about dragonflies. The red dragonflies (aka tombo) that appear in these poems refer to dragonflies of the genus *Sympetrum*, commonly referred to as meadowhawks in North America, as darters in Europe. These are common late season dragonflies and, in traditional Japanese poetry, a symbol of autumn.

Ken Tennessen and I have traveled the haiku road together for several years now, both on the page and in the field. The haiku in this book began after a day walking logging trails in northern Minnesota in search of dragonflies as part of our work for the Minnesota Odonata Survey Project (now the Minnesota Dragonfly Society). On that particular summer day in 2012, we were looking for the uncommon species known as Emeralds, large dragonflies with astonishingly green eyes, endemic to boreal bogs and peatlands. The following two haiku relate to that day:

> Like Basho and Sora long ago
> taking the narrow road to the interior
> Ken and I, also, battle deer flies.

> Overgrown logging road,
> a torment of deer flies, but the wolf tracks
> lead us to orchids and emeralds

At some point we began sharing our haiku through email. Occasionally one haiku would prompt another, or a back-and-forth volley would ensue with further haiku written in response.

While presumptuous to hold our haiku up to those of a master such as Issa, we felt justified in creating this collection to pay tribute to these wonderful insects we've spent so much time admiring. Hopefully, in spite of any flaws and limitations in the text, these haiku will deepen the experience of other readers and other observers of dragonflies. If this collection succeeds in that one goal, both Ken and I shall be very pleased.

One final bow to Issa. One final bow to my comrade,
Ken. One final bow to the dragonflies.

– Scott King
Northfield, December 2015

A note on the translations

These new versions are shaped by my experience with
the natural history of dragonflies and only the most
rudimentary knowledge of Japanese. Most importantly,
these versions would not have existed without the
extraordinary work done by David Lanoue who has
translated 10,000 of Issa's haiku and made them available
in a searchable archive at haikuguy.com. So I humbly
present these new versions of Issa with ten thousand
bows to David and highly recommend his two critical
studies *Pure Land Haiku: The Art of Priest Issa* and *Issa
and the Meaning of Animals: A Buddhist Poet's Perspective*
and his generous collection of Issa's haiku *Issa's Best: A
Translator's Selection of Master Haiku.*

Further Reading

Jean Henri Fabre. *The Passionate Observer*. Chronicle Books. 1998

Robert Hass (ed.) *The Essential Haiku: Versions of Basho, Buson, and Issa*. Ecco Press. 1994

Kobayashi Issa. Issa's Best: A Translator's Selection of Master Haiku. David G. Lanoue. 2012

Lafcadio Hearn. *Dragonflies*. Red Dragonfly Press. 2016

Kobayashi Issa. *The Spring of My Life: And Selected Haiku*. Sam Hamill, translator. Shambhala. 1997.

David Lanoue. *Issa and the Meaning of Animals: A Buddhist Poet's Perspective*. David G. Lanoue. 2014

David Lanoue. *Pure Land Haiku: The Art of Priest Issa*. David G. Lanoue. 2004; 2nd E-book Edition 2013

Ian Marshall. *Walden by Haiku*. University of Georgia Press. 2009

Harry Martinson. *Views from a Tuft of Grass*. Green Integer. 2005

Bruce Ross (ed.). *Haiku Moment: An Anthology of Contemporary North American Haiku*. Tuttle. 1993

Bart Sutter. *Chester Creek Ravine: Haiku*. Nodin Press. 2015

Gerald Vizenor. *Favor of Crows: New and Selected Haiku*. Wesleyan University Press. 2014

Kobayashi Issa

ANNOTATED HAIKU

ばん石にかぢり付たるとんぼ哉

banjaku ni kajiritsuketaru tombo kana

Midstream
clinging to a boulder—
the dragonfly

See note on following page.

ばん石にかぢり付たるとんぼ哉

banjaku ni kajiritsuketaru tombo kana

Gripping
an immense rock—
the dragonfly

A second version of the poem from the previous page.
Both scenarios are common and I'm not at all certain
which Issa had in mind. Skimmer dragonflies often
perch on rocks for warmth and as a platform to hunt
off from. Clubtail dragonflies are often found on rocks
in the middle of streams and rivers. Either way, I believe
this poem has to do with attachment; Issa seems to be
chiding the dragonfly for being so attached to worldly
things. [1816]

蜻蛉や二尺飛では又二尺

tombō ya ni shaku tonde wa mata ni shaku

Stupid dragonfly!
flying two feet and landing, then
two feet more, two feet more...

Often, when first disturbed, a dragonfly will fly only a
short distance away. Issa obviously finds this behavior
humorous, given how easy it would be for the dragonfly
to fly a great distance, or perhaps he's simply amused by
the dragonfly's laziness. [1804]

蜻蛉の百度参りやあたご山

tombō no hyakudo mairi ya atago yama

The dragonfly
takes off one hundred times
for Mount Atago Temple

I take this to be an observation of a perched dragonfly,
one that leaves its perch, flying out and returning, over
and over. Issa makes the connection to the curious local
tradition of walking prayers, during which the pilgrim
either visits the temple on one hundred consecutive
days, or completes a circuit between a particular place
and the temple one hundred times. [date unknown]

朝寒もはや合点のとんぼ哉

asa-zamu mo haya gatten no tombo kana

Cold morning
slow to get out of bed
the dragonfly

One of the great perks that comes with studying
dragonflies is not having to get out of bed early, as
dragonflies don't begin to fly until the sun is out and the
day is warm. I believe Issa approved of this lazy behavior
as being in harmony with his own laziness, especially on
cold mornings. The last line could just as well read "the
dragonfly and I." [1808]

蜻蛉の尻でなぶるや角田川

tombō no shiri de naburu ya sumida-gawa

The dragonfly
artfully tapping the water—
Sumida River

The behavior depicted in this haiku is of a dragonfly
depositing eggs into the river. The haiku seems to
suggest that the dragonfly might be playing in the water,
maybe even scribbling on the water surface a few lines
of verse. Another possibility, given Issa's propensity for
capturing all aspects of life no matter how low, is that
the dragonfly is bathing its private parts in the river. The
Sumida River runs through Tokyo. [1813]

我門に煤びた色のとんぼ哉

waga kado [ni] susubita iro no tombo kana

How fitting!
the one dragonfly at my gate
the color of soot

An example of Issa's self-deprecating nature. No doubt
at every other gate is a brightly colored dragonfly,
blue or red or gold. But Issa, poor Issa, who is such an
admirer of dragonflies, finds only one and its color
is that of dirt or soot. But, more importantly, Issa is
content with this dragonfly, not drawn in to the pursuit
of the more showy varieties to be found elsewhere.
[1816]

御祭の赤い出立の蜻蛉哉

o-matsuri no akai dedachi no tombo kana

Ready for the festival
dressed to the nines!
red dragonfly

There is both admiration and ridicule here, I think. The
dragonfly is beautiful, but still, the clothes might betray
the putting on of airs, especially in the eyes of this poor,
poet-priest. [1817]

御仏の代におぶさる蜻蛉哉

mi-botoke no kawari ni obusaru tombo kana

From my shoulder
to the Buddha's shoulder—
the dragonfly

The last dragonfly to be observed in Minnesota,
surviving past the first hard freeze and often past the
first snowfall, is the Autumn Meadowhawk. In October
and November, if you stand in the sun near where these
dragonflies congregate, one will eventually land on your
shoulder, or your legs, or your belly. When they fly away,
I think of this poem. There is a connection here between
poet and the divine, the dragonfly is a reminder, and a
guide pointing Issa, and us, toward the Pure Land. [1818]

蜻蛉やはったとにらむふじの山

tombō ya hatta to niramu fuji no yama

The dragonfly —
who can stare longer
at Mount Fuji?

Issa was fascinated by the compound eyes of
dragonflies — and who can blame him, as those large,
unblinking orbs are certainly one of their most striking
features. When you watch a dragonfly for a long period
of time, especially one that is perched, it's natural to
wonder about their vision. What does the world look
like through their eyes? How do they sleep? *Do* they
sleep? and so on. At least four other poems by Issa have
the dragonfly staring or glowering — at the Buddha, at
the moon, at another mountain, through the rain. [1825]

俳人を済度に入れるか赤とんぼ

haijin wo saido ni ireru ka aka tombō

Red dragonfly —
are you here to lead us
to enlightenment?

Here, the red dragonfly is given high status indeed — its
sudden appearance likened to the visitation of a god. It
is a godsend. It can save us if we let it, leading us to the
Pure Land. The "us" has been translated variously as
"haiku poets" and "criminals" — I've gone with the more
general term, intending something like "any of us" or
"us poor, non-attentive human beings." [1823]

Kobayashi Issa

HAIKU

The red dragonfly
not overly worried about
the cold snap

Days are short —
the dragonfly's life
fleeting as well

Poor dragonfly
even your slender abdomen
grows gray

The red dragonfly
also enjoys the view
of sunset

Dusk shadows
flood the grass — at the very tip
the red dragonfly

On the receiving end
of the dragonfly's stern look—
the Buddha

Crinkly crunch—
the dragonfly nymph's
empty skin

Unblinking eyes
gaze through the rain storm—
the dragonfly

At rice-harvest time
the dragonfly, hands together,
also knows how to pray

Drinking her fill
of clear, morning dew
the dragonfly

Emerging dragonfly —
climbing out of itself
headfirst

Dragonflies
mistaken for fallen leaves —
Tatsuta River

Dragonflies
flying back-and-forth like shuttles
through a loom

At the very top
of the flag pole
a dragonfly

Motionless all night
scowling at the sliver of moon
the dragonfly

Vacating the premises
both butterfly and dragonfly —
the fart bug

A dragonfly
asleep on the antlers
of the deer

Beneath the hotel eaves
a dragonfly checks in quickly —
travelling alone

Darting and hovering
near the horse's ears —
gossiping dragonfly

Against the black fence
the dragonfly believes
it's well hidden

Ken Tennessen

HAIKU

The path
of a dragonfly
cannot be followed

Spring peepers
announce
the dragonfly

The path winding
ever skyward
is the dragonfly's

Turn back
if you're lost
on the dragonfly's path

Spring comes—
the dragonfly is back
on its path

The only thing
that can follow a dragonfly
is another dragonfly

Crawling off the edge
of winter—
a dragonfly nymph

The red dragonfly,
eye-catching, but not looking for
admiration

Concentric ripples
in the middle of the pond—
dragonfly tapping

Dragonflies show us
how to be
free

Blue damselfly
slowly munched —
green dragonfly

Dragonfly nymphs
in the warm waters of spring
ready to uncoil

Somatochlora
emerging from the sphagnum —
purely bog-mindling

Wary dragonfly
talks not to the scientist
but to the poet

In the creek's shallows
a Doe drinks, legs encircled
by a Fawn Darner

Inside the camper
mosquitoes buzz sleepy ears —
dragonflies missed some!

Darkness creeping . . .
dragonflies hanging up,
no hugs goodnight

Odonate way:
three hundred million years
of aerial sex

All-day rain —
not one dragonfly
to be seen

A blade of grass
that avoids my tramping feet?
No! Eastern Pondhawk

Blue Pond Damsel
snared in a spider web . . .
I am helpless

I long to step back
to the Carboniferous,
see the griffinflies

A darner exuvia
clinging to a cattail stem
as if still alive

Chill of morning—
like a dragonfly, I welcome
the rising sun

Sweet summer rain
filling a parched swale—
spreadwings waiting

Wild dragonfly
showing me how
to be free

Green Darners southbound —
don't know where
they'll be tomorrow

Sun-up dragonfly,
wings dew-laden.
Will you fly again?

Fawn Darners
lending some light
to the dying day

From deep water
a dragonfly emerges.
It has new eyes

Yesterday's song
afloat—
a dead dragonfly

Male Jewelwings
test their metal
over water

Clubtails
on the Chippewa —
countless

Three days of hard rain . . .
under bent grass blades —
hungry damselflies

On a Flambeau bridge
I watched a river cruiser
disappear downstream

Scott King

HAIKU

The first dragonfly of the year—
almost too fast
for out-of-practice eyes

The first dragonfly
passes by so swiftly — everything else
seems set in stone

Bright red bookmark
placed on the first page of spring —
the migrant dragonfly

The season changes
unfolds itself over open water —
the first baskettail

Winter wears on and on —
the memory of dragonflies gets lost
in the spring snowstorm

Too far north!
snowflakes striking pastel eyes
the migrant dragonfly

Ink glistening
on morning's damp page —
a new dragonfly!

Poor, silly dragonfly —
not able to tell a rose
from a stick

Red Dragonfly
what could you be thinking
perched on my fingertip?

Ach dragonfly! Are ye daft—
preferring a deid stick
to a blooming flouer!?

Now look at that—
the clever dragonfly pretending
to sniff that flower

Overhead at dusk
searching invisible labyrinths
the blue dragonflies

Out of breath
at the top of the steep hill—
a dragonfly goes by

Above the pond
cork-screwing toward heaven
two dragonflies

Hung up to dry
a fresh painting on damp paper —
the new dragonfly

That pestering deer fly
suddenly gone — captured by
the dragonfly

The wiggling mosquito larvae
vanishes in a flash — snatched by
the damselfly nymph

At the bottom of the pond,
suddenly one size larger—
the dragonfly nymph

Embarrassed—
the red dragonfly not yet red
hiding in the bushes

Some kind of answer—
at the edge of the sunlit pond
dressed in dragonflies!

A ray of sunlight
aslant a fallen leaf—
red dragonfly

Clamped in the Kingbird's bill —
still searching the blue sky
the dragonfly

The dragonfly —
here to show us the way to heaven
and earth

Bright-sun-flashing-wings—
instead of ice on the pond
November dragonflies!

Staring past
the one staring at it—
the red dragonfly

The thinnest shadow
causes it to fly away —
the red dragonfly

Holding tight
to the car's antenna —
three migrating dragonflies

The Dragonhunter
alone on the nameless shore
hot July evening

A dragonfly wing
impressed in shoreline mud—
all that's left of the day's thought

Up late at the Baudette Motel —
under bright lights in new rooms
we study ancient insects

The Fawn Darner flits like a bat.
I swing my net like a fool — no dragonfly,
but Voila! a bright green frog.

The boat ramp in Warroad
cars, boats, families jangle in the sun —
I bend down to study a blue damselfly

At the Rainy River
a clubtail crosses from Canada
and lands at my feet

Unnoticed
Black Meadowhawks with fresh wings
sparkle in the morning sun

Several nights in a row
we drink and eat at Rosalee's Diner
talking dragonflies

Overgrown logging road,
a torment of deer flies, but the wolf tracks
lead us to orchids and emeralds

Not quite a poem,
the camera capturing only the image —
red dragonfly on green leaf

Working patiently
to net an elusive dragonfly —
an otter swims by

The red dragonfly
a small amount of sunset
trapped in its wings

Only three wings!
yet the autumn dragonfly flies on
without a limp

The elusive dragonfly
glides past your ankles easy as the river —
forget the net, use your pen!

Too many black flies,
way too many deer flies. Hey dragonflies
what are you waiting for?

No mosquitoes,
no deer flies, and no black flies—
but no dragonflies either

Museum dragonfly
stuck on that pin for fifty years
dusty as a model airplane

Chasing dragonflies—
I stop to pick handfuls of wild
black raspberries

One dragonfly —
even the most silent of ponds
comes alive

So many meetings
first one dragonfly, then another
so many goodbyes

Kobayashi Issa (1763 - 1828), a lay priest of Shin Buddhism (the True Pure Land School), wrote over 20,000 haiku and is considered one of the great Japanese masters of the form.

Ken Tennessen is the author of *Waushara County Dragonflies and Damselflies* (guidebook), *Utterly Bugged* (Red Dragonfy Press, 2013) and numerous scientific articles about dragonflies. He calls Wisconsin home but travels widely, mostly researching and photographing dragonflies.

Scott King is a poet and citizen scientist who lives in Northfield, Minnesota. In addition to being editor of Red Dragonfly Press, he's been researching the dragonflies of the genus *Sympetrum* (the red dragonflies) in preparation of a book on their natural history.

Made in the USA
Middletown, DE
02 August 2022

70416389R00066